WHAT'S INSIDE A Remote Control?

![The Child's World logo] The Child's World®
childsworld.com

Published by The Child's World®
1980 Lookout Drive • Mankato, MN 56003-1705
800-599-READ • www.childsworld.com

Photographs ©: Rick Orndorf, cover (remote), 1 (remote), 4, 7, 9, 10 (remote), 11 (remote cover), 13 (top), 13 (bottom), 15, 17 (top), 17 (bottom), 19, 24; Shutterstock Images, cover (circuit board), cover (bulb), 1 (circuit board), 1 (bulb), 2, 3 (circuit board), 3 (plug), 5 (glasses), 6 (bulb), 6 (circuit board), 10 (buttons), 11 (circuit board), 14 (circuit board), 16, 18 (buttons), 20 (circuit board), 21, 22, 23 (buttons); Oleksandr Kostiuchenko/Shutterstock Images, cover (batteries), 1 (batteries), 12 (batteries), 14 (batteries), 20 (batteries); Praiwun Thungsarn/Shutterstock Images, 3 (screwdriver), 5 (screwdriver), 8, 12 (screwdriver), 18 (screwdriver), 23 (screwdriver); Shyripa Alexandr/Shutterstock Images, 5 (gloves)

ISBN 9781503832350
LCCN 2018963090

Printed in the United States of America
PA02419

About the Author

Arnold Ringstad lives in Minnesota. He uses a remote control every time he watches TV.

Contents

Materials and Safety

Materials

- ☐ Remote control
- ☐ Safety glasses
- ☐ Screwdriver
- ☐ Work gloves

Safety

- Remove the batteries from the remote control before taking it apart.

- Be careful when handling sharp objects, such as screwdrivers.

- Wear work gloves to protect your hands from sharp edges.

- Wear safety glasses in case pieces snap off.

Remote control

Work gloves

Screwdriver

Safety glasses

Inside a
Remote Control

Many people like to watch TV. But they don't want to get up to change the channel. To solve this problem, engineers invented the remote control. You can control the TV or DVD player from your couch or chair. How does a remote control work? What's inside?

Back

Circuit board

Button sheet

Battery cover

Front

Opening the Remote

The back of the remote is attached to the front. Small plastic tabs hold the two pieces together. You can use the screwdriver to pry them apart. Pull the front piece off. Underneath you will see the flexible sheet of buttons.

Safety Note

The screwdriver is sharp, so be careful when prying open the remote.

The flexible sheet of buttons sits just below the hard plastic front.

Under the Cover

This remote works with a DVD player. Its buttons do many things. One turns the player on or off.

The buttons are labeled with numbers, symbols, or words.

Some labels are on the cover instead of the buttons.

One button opens the DVD player's disc tray. Other buttons turn the volume up or down. Some buttons are labeled on the flexible sheet. Others have labels on the hard plastic front cover.

Making Contact

Pull the flexible plastic sheet away. Below it is a **circuit board**. For every button, there are flat metal lines that do not touch. On the plastic sheet, each button has a small metal disc. Pressing a button makes the metal disc touch the metal lines. This lets electricity flow.

Safety Note

The edges of the circuit board may be sharp. Be careful when handling it.

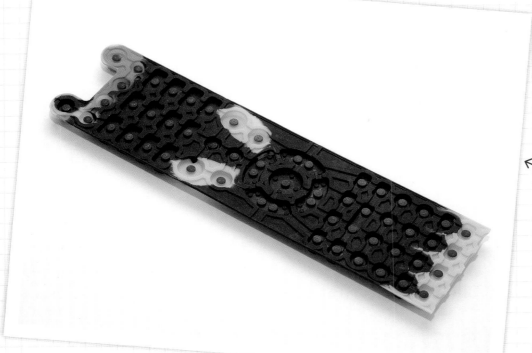

The flexible sheet has a small metal disc below each button.

Each button has metal lines under it that do not touch.

Getting Power

The remote's electricity comes from batteries. The batteries are in the back. A small door covers them. They send electricity into the circuit board. The electricity travels through the flat metal lines.

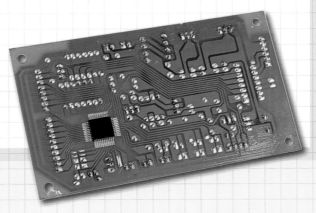

Springs

Springs help hold the batteries in place.

Lighting Up

When electricity flows through a circuit board, a **microchip** on the back of the circuit board creates a signal. That signal goes to a **light-emitting diode** (LED) at the top of the remote. The LED sends out **infrared** light. People cannot see this light. But a special **detector** on the DVD player can.

The LED's light can't be seen by human eyes.

A tiny microchip creates signals for the remote to send.

Sending Signals

The LED flashes on and off in different patterns. Each button has its own pattern. When the DVD player's detector sees the pattern for "volume up," it turns the volume up. The remote also sends a signal that says which device it is for. That way the DVD player does not respond to the wrong remote.

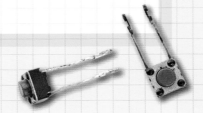

Detector on the DVD player's circuit board

Reusing a
Remote Control

We've taken apart a remote control
and learned what's inside. Now
what? Here are some ideas for
how to reuse the parts of a remote
control. Can you think of any more?

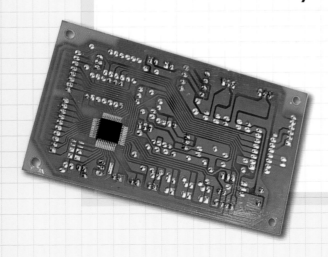

- **Bookmark:** The remote control has a long, flat circuit board. If you pull the battery contacts off it, you can use it as a bookmark!

- **Invisible Lights:** Human eyes cannot see infrared light, but cell phone cameras can! In a dark room, use a phone camera to watch the LED while you press buttons. You can see the LED flash!

Glossary

circuit board (SUR-kit BORD): A circuit board is a piece of material that holds computer chips, switches, and other parts. Inside the remote control, a circuit board holds the circuits that are underneath each button.

detector (di-TEK-tur): A detector is something that notices or receives something, such as a signal. A DVD player's detector receives the signals that the remote control sends.

infrared (in-fruh-RED): Infrared light is a kind of light that people cannot see. The remote flashes infrared light to send signals to the DVD player.

light-emitting diode (LITE-i-MIT-ing DY-ohd): A light-emitting diode (LED) is a small electronic part that creates light. An LED in the remote sends signals using infrared light.

microchip (MY-kroh-chip): A microchip is a part that contains electrical circuits designed to do a certain job. In a remote control, the microchip creates signals to send to the LED.

To Learn More

IN THE LIBRARY

Holzweiss, Kristina. *Amazing Makerspace DIY with Electricity*. New York, NY: Scholastic, 2018.

Mattern, Joanne. *Remote Control Planes*. New York, NY: Children's Press, 2016.

Ringstad, Arnold. *What's Inside a Remote-Controlled Car?* Mankato, MN: The Child's World, 2020.

ON THE WEB

Visit our website for links about taking apart a remote control: **childsworld.com/links**

Note to Parents, Teachers, and Librarians: We routinely verify our Web links to make sure they are safe and active sites. So encourage your readers to check them out!

Index